THIS WALKER BOOK BELONGS TO:

_____

_____

_____

_____

First published 1986 by Walker Books Ltd
87 Vauxhall Walk, London SE11 5HJ

This edition published 1998

2 4 6 8 10 9 7 5 3

© 1986 Colin & Jacqui Hawkins

Printed in Hong Kong/China

British Library Cataloguing in Publication Data
A catalogue record for this book is
available from the British Library.

ISBN 0-7445-6096-9 J|1686381

JUNGLE
SOUNDS

Colin and Jacqui Hawkins

WALKER BOOKS
AND SUBSIDIARIES
LONDON • BOSTON • SYDNEY

Mmm, I just love butterflies.

A panther
can...

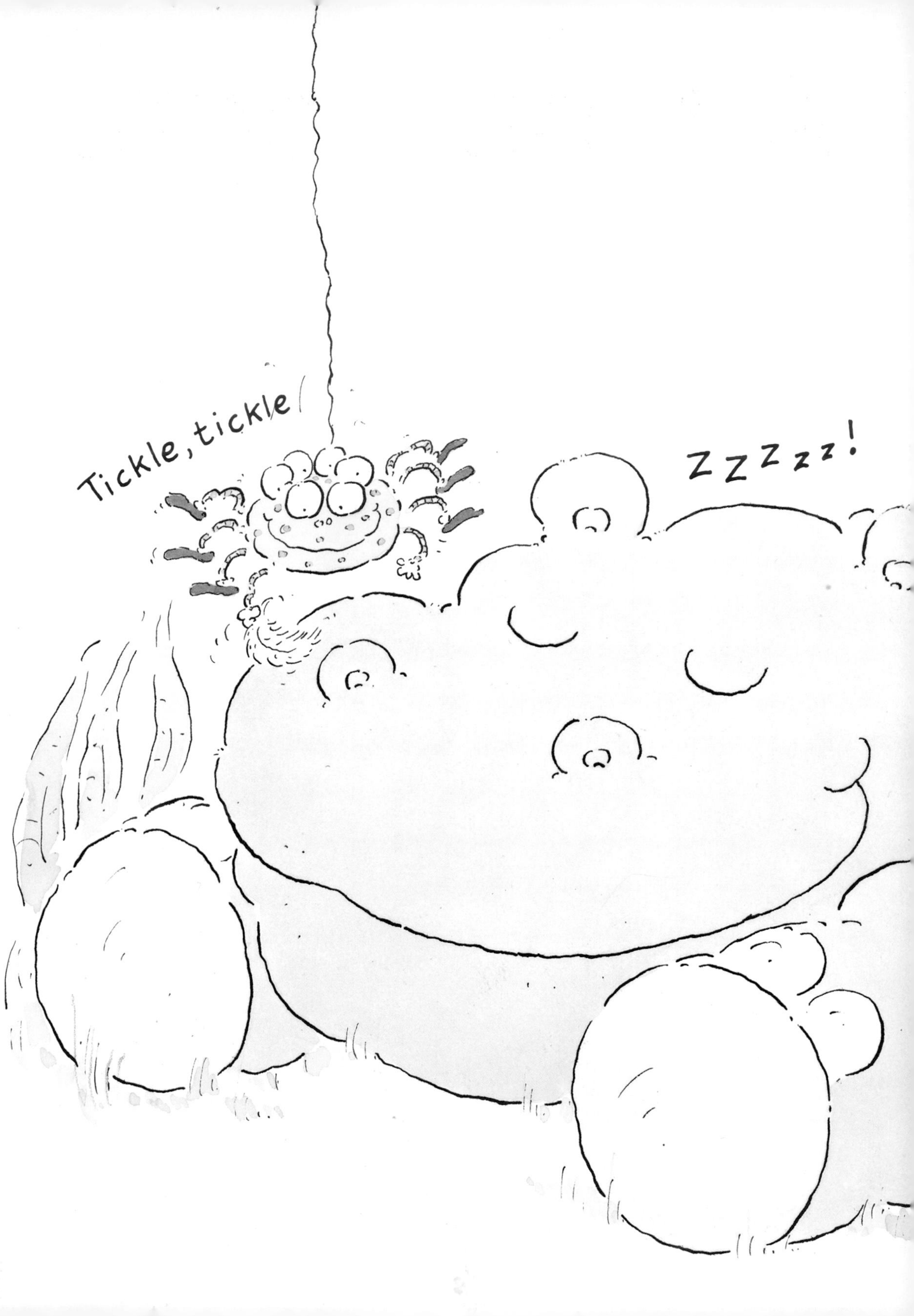
Tickle, tickle
ZZZzzz!

A hippo can…

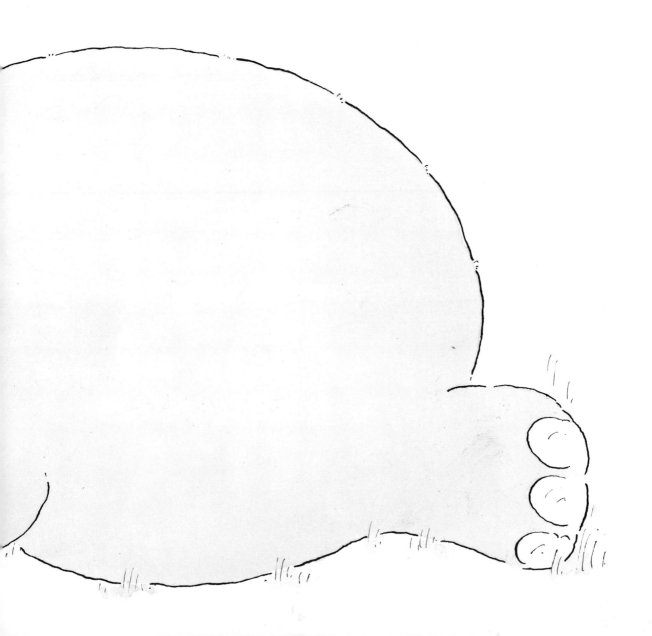

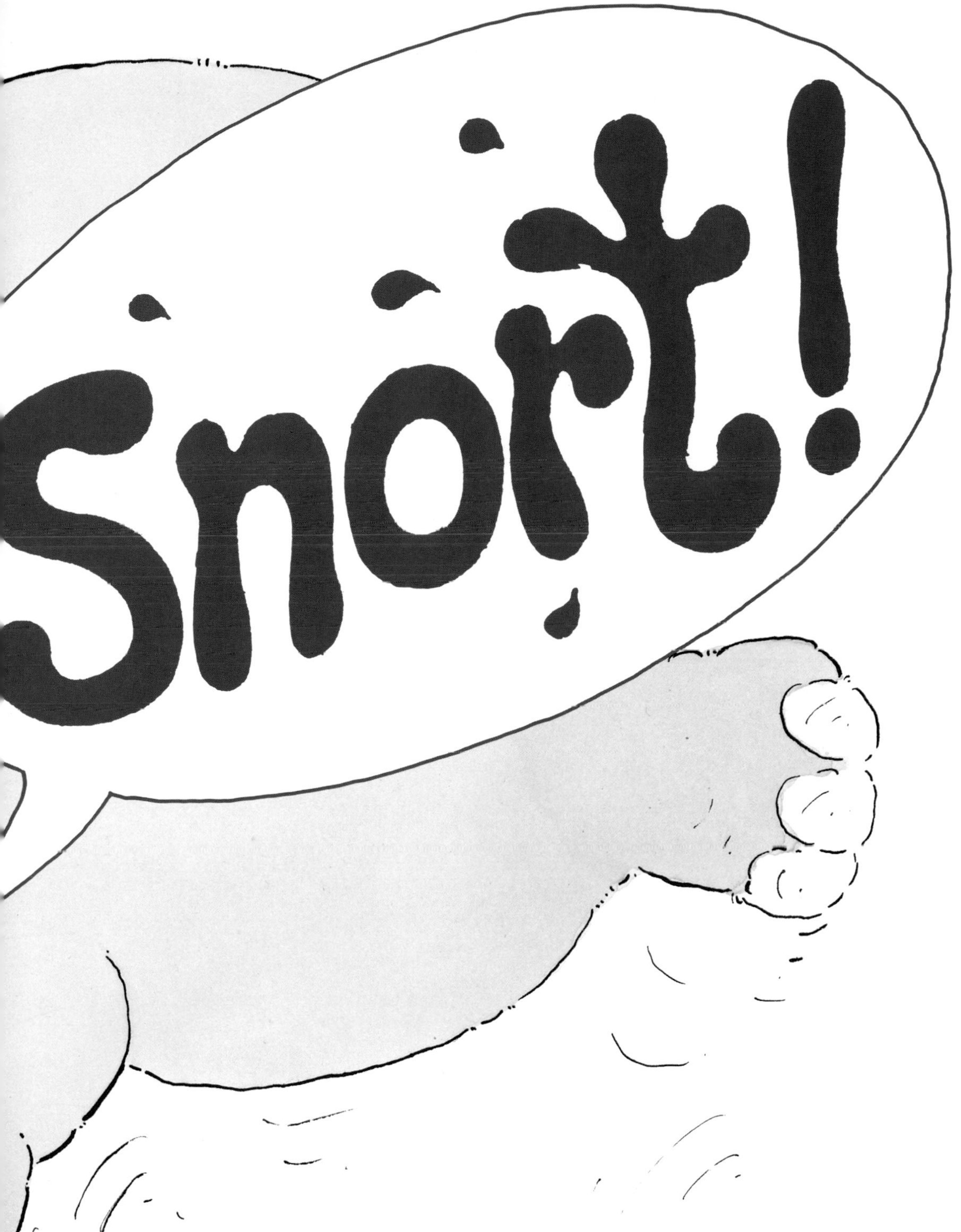
Snort!

A crocodile will...

Silly old crocodile!

I do like flowers.

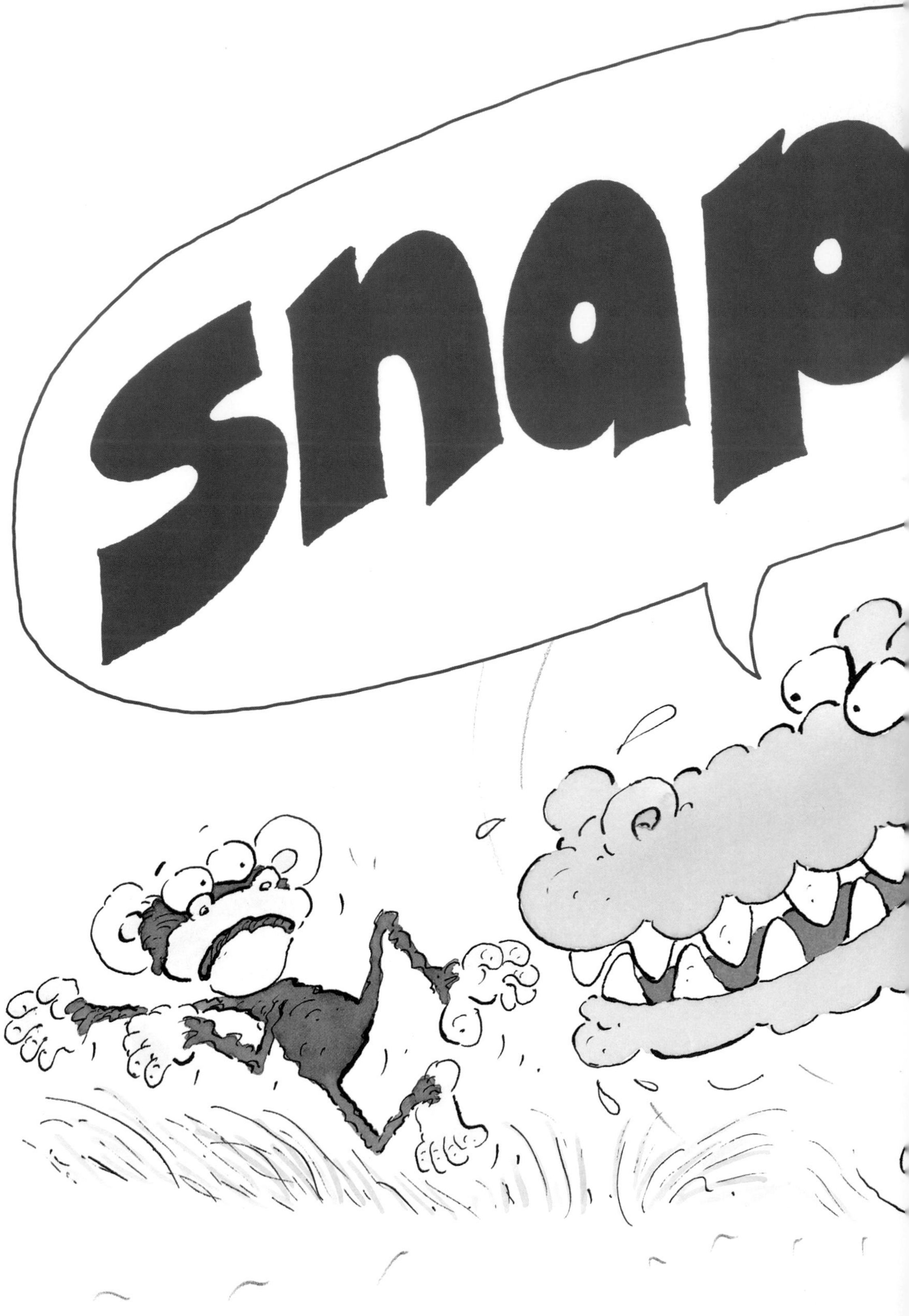
snap

Where did I put that honey?

A bear might...

A tiger will...

Oooh!
What a nice
fat caterpillar!

And a snake will...

Go on. Kiss him.
I dare you!

Kiss! Kiss!

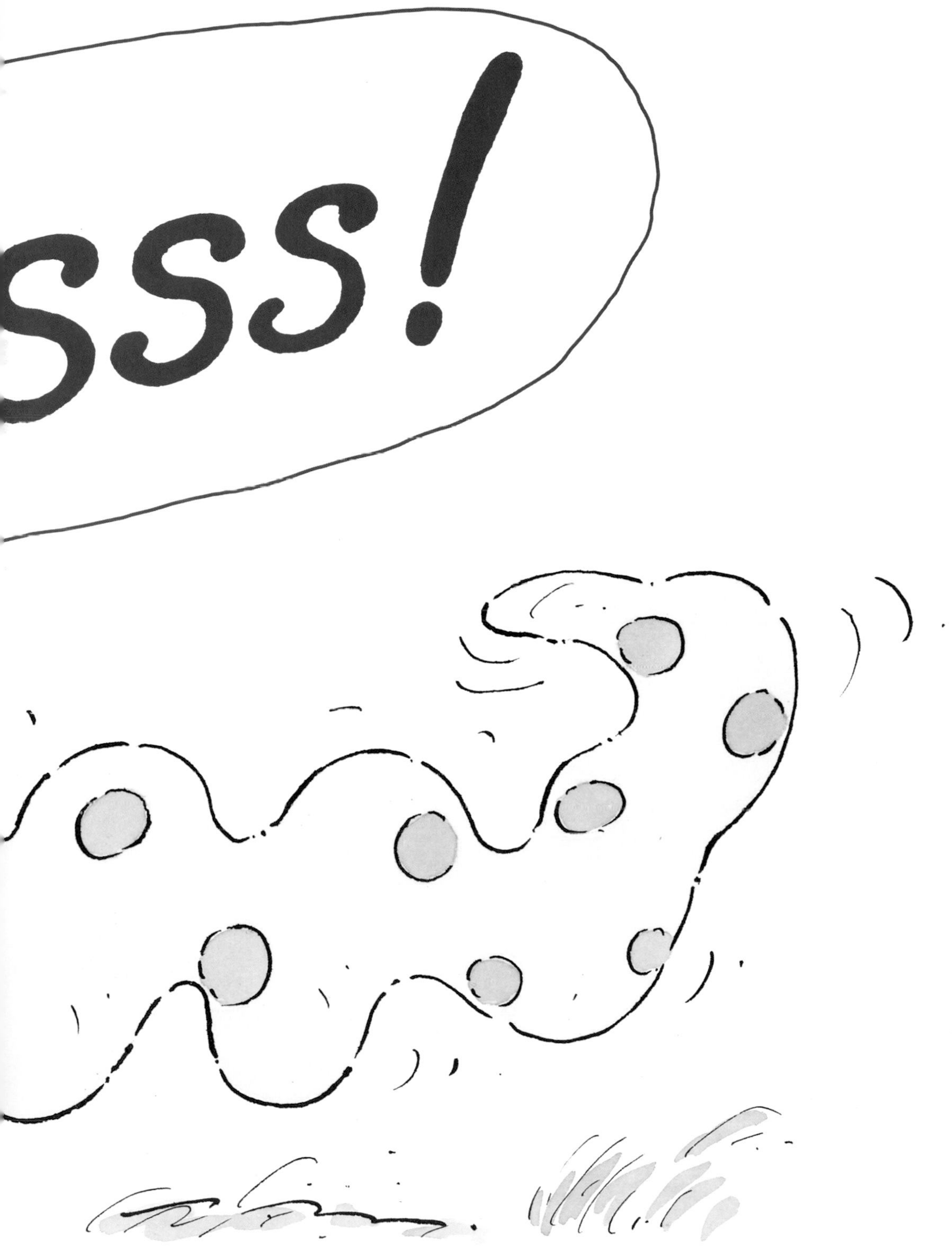
sss!

How many jungle sounds

can you make like this?

MORE WALKER PAPERBACKS
For You to Enjoy

Also by Colin and Jacqui Hawkins

FARMYARD SOUNDS

Neigh! Baa! Quack! Moo!

How many farm sounds can you do?

Another book of noisy animal
fun for the very young.

0-7445-6095-0   £4.50

TERRIBLE, TERRIBLE TIGER

A wonderfully entertaining rhyming picture book about
a tiger who is not quite what he seems!

0-7445-5230-3   £4.50

THE WIZARD'S CAT

An energetic and amusing rhyming picture book about a cat
who wishes he were something else!

0-7445-5231-1   £4.50